ONLY IN AMERICA

Case For: Immigration And International Human Rights

AF885475

KEEPING FAMILIES TOGETHER

By **Martin V. Asatrian, Esq.**

Speakeasy Publishing
73-03 Bell Blvd, #10
Oakland Gardens, NY 11364
www.speakeasypublishinginc.com

Ordering Information:

Quantity sales. Special discounts are available on quantity purchases by corporations, associations, and others. For details, contact the publisher at the address above.

Orders by U.S. trade bookstores and wholesalers. Please contact Speakeasy Publishing: Tel: (888) 991-2766 or visit www.speakeasypublishinginc.com.

Printed in the United States of America.

Published in 2017.

ISBN: 978-1-946481-09-2

FOREWORD

Why did I write this book? Well, most people write books usually for one reason; a fear of death. They want something concrete to have when they die or something to leave behind that simply documents their short time here on earth. They want to leave a unique or perceived unique point of your life. This book is choppy at best but that is what I like about it. It's an autobiography with a twist. The twist is my life and this book is not unique and anyone reading this book should write their own as well. Everyone has an interesting life and they are all around us. We are usually preoccupied with "important" things and don't bother to look and ask questions.

I found great joy in writing this book because it allowed me to reflect on my life and what I have accomplished and on what I have not accomplished. It was basically a "time out" from the fast paced world around us and it helped me share some of my disjointed experiences in life. I am thankful to all those that read this book and encourage them to write their own. We all need a "time out" from life to meditate and reflect on its wonder.

As I get older, I reflect more and more on my surroundings. I rigorously question things. I doubt myself, but I am amazed how as a people we are so resilient; how we adapt to change so well. This is really a book on being eternally optimistic about the world and at the same time an expression of worry about how we have become less sensitive as citizens towards immigrants. I make a case for why the U.S. without question has benefited enormously from the wave of immigration to come to our shore. The fundamental point is that the immigrant spirit is the human spirit. The spirit stated simply is to strive for a better life. What is a better life? A life where you can raise a family, work hard, and be judged on your merits. Sure people are going to be better off than you at birth with talent or with their trust fund. It does not matter. The name of the game is to value the freedom, and not measure success by how much money you have, or don't have. Rather it should be measured by your sense of tranquility and freedom to work hard or not. We all can use some of the energy, innovation, and resilience immigrants teach us every day. The 'American Spirit' has always been the kindness of strangers. All I am advocating in this book, "Only in America" is that as a country, we have an amazing ability to show kindness and compassion in our short journey, to strangers. We have only just begun. So many immigrants, refugees, and undocumented individuals have contributed to the fabric of our country so let us embrace the "stranger" and learn from them; their spirit, fearlessness, and willingness to get the job done.

Mass deportations have never been the answer from a historical standpoint. The American story is about assimilation. United we stand; divided we fall. Unity of people from different parts of the world makes the United States the shiny city on the hill. So let us keep the promise to each other and be kind to the other; to strangers, to immigrants, and to refugees. Uniting families and uniting our nation are inseparable notions. Thank you for your time in reading this short book.

Author: M.V.A.

DEDICATION

Where do I start? I dedicate this book to my son, a beautiful boy, Benjamin Barkev Asatrian. He is the light of my life. I also dedicate this book to the memory of my father, Barkev Asatrian. I am not sure how many people will read this book but it will be made available to my four-year-old as he matures to understand a little of his family history.

DISCLAIMER

This publication is intended to be used for educational purposes only. No legal advice is being given, and no attorney-client relationship is intended to be created by reading this material. The author assumes no liability for any errors or omissions or for how this book or its contents are used or interpreted or for any consequences resulting directly or indirectly from the use of this book. For legal or any other advice, please consult an experienced attorney or the appropriate expert.

Asatrian Law Group, LLC
1047 Anderson Avenue
Fort Lee, NJ 07024
(201) 663-3164
www.AsatrianLawGroup.com

TABLE OF CONTENTS

About The Author

Martin V. Asatrian is a founding and managing partner of the Asatrian Law Group, LLC with an office headquartered in Fort Lee, New Jersey 07024. He has obtained substantial verdicts throughout his career. He obtained his college degree from New York University and his law degree from New York Law School. He has also obtained a certificate of International Law from Oxford University, United Kingdom.

Mr. Asatrian was elected to the Englewood Cliffs Council where he served as the Police Commissioner. He was previously a named partner of the prestigious law firm of Weiner Lesniak, LLC and served as Of Counsel at the Sekas Law Group, LLC. He has taught as an adjunct professor at William Paterson University, Bergen Community College, and Essex County College. He is a proud member of the Board of Directors of the Greater Fort Lee Chamber of Commerce. He is an active member of the ABA Standing Committee on National Security Law. He is an active member of the community and was a former board member of the Society for Orphaned Armenian Relief Society.

PRACTICE AREAS:

1. PERSONAL INJURY
   - Truck Accidents
   - Construction Accidents
   - Negligent Security
   - Burn Injury
   - Workplace Accidents
   - Motorcycle Accidents
   - Slips and Falls
   - Dog Bites
   - Forklift Accidents
   - Hit and Run Accidents

2. EMPLOYMENT LAW
   - Discrimination
   - Retaliation
   - Sexual Harassment
   - Negotiate Separation Agreements
   - Non-Compete Agreements

3. COMMERCIAL LITIGATION
   - Business Contracts and Agreements
   - Business Transactions
   - Business Litigation and Disputes

The Author With His Son Beniamin

CHAPTER 1
WHY DO YOU PRACTICE PERSONAL INJURY LAW?

I grew up in the very blue-collar town of Fairview, New Jersey. My dad was a yellow cab driver in fact. In the 7th grade, I wrote a book report on what career path I wanted to take. Even then, I wanted to be a lawyer. What drove me to law was probably a little misconceived at the time. The lawyers that I knew of, as an eleven-year-old eager kid, were the ones that had a lot of power. I respected them and I was seduced by it.

Even so, I knew it took much more than that. I had to have much more education on the law. Coming from my background, it probably would explain why I chose to focus on personal injury and immigration. They both involved enormous amounts of pain and suffering. As a child, I always wanted to be the voice to the silent and to help those that needed it. I was too proud to ask for help. So as a young adolescent, that was the direction I was led in.

What Has Shaped You To Be The Man And The Attorney That You Are Today?

When you look to hire an attorney you are not necessarily going to know or care a whole lot about their personal background. My background, however, is somewhat enlightening and reflects on who I am today and how I practice law. I was born in Armenia, which at the time was the Soviet Armenia; part of the larger Soviet Union bloc.

My father was a butcher at the time and I remember going to the farm on the weekends. One of my oldest memories from that time in Armenia, was the KGB once approaching my father. He was taken to the police station and interrogated. I don't remember why that happened exactly but I do recall the look on my father's face; the look of fear, anxiety, and worry.

At that time, the Soviet Union was going through a hard time. There was talk of getting rid of the Russian Jews, the ethnic Armenians, and some of the ethnic Germans at that time. Luckily my father had a sister in the United States who had petitioned for us. We were fortunate enough to get out of the Soviet Union and come to the U.S. in the legal status of the refugee, which should be distinguished from coming here as an immigrant.

At the time most émigrés, including my family, went from the Soviet Union to Rome for six months on our way to the U.S. We needed to be civilized in a European country before we came over.

We had no money as we weren't allowed to bring any money out of the Soviet Union. Therefore my family went through many different and trying experiences. We sold trinkets at flea markets at the Vatican and that sort of thing to get by. None of this ever made us unhappy. The family unit was all together and that is what kept the smiles on our faces. That was our experience crossing into the United States.

Tough Experiences Help Build Strong Character

If things went wrong and the KGB had arrested my dad, he would have had to serve a five-year jail term. Our mother would then have raised us while my dad was in prison. That made a strong imprint on my mind about the fear of the government back then. When we came to the United States, we had very little money. However, we had an enormous amount of optimism. We were amazed by how plentiful the United States was.

We initially moved into North Bergen, New Jersey and then on to Fairview, New Jersey, a blue-collar town. It impacted my life a great deal. My dad began working as a dishwasher, and we eventually saved up some money, and bought a hot dog truck. I used to go with him in those early days. We sold hot dogs to make money in order to pay our rent, which was $175 a month back in 1979. We didn't know we were poor; we just knew we had a great family. My mom unfortunately worked at a sweatshop at the time and knew nothing else; it was month-to-month, week to week. No matter what, my dad always bought us donuts on Saturdays. That I remember well. He is deceased now and that's why I talk and remember him so fondly.

If there is any takeaway from this book, it's to cherish every moment with your parents. Someday they will not be around and you may have to write these type of books like I am doing now. As a parent myself, I have learned to appreciate my parents more; the sacrifices, the fearlessness, the love. It's amazing how parents sacrifice everything for their children.

The Author

CHAPTER 2
HOW DID YOU END UP AS A PERSONAL INJURY AND IMMIGRATION ATTORNEY?

Some of my great teachers always told me in high school that the key to escaping poverty, or just the lower middle-class, is education. They actually said the way was through education or the military. I chose education. I was not a great student in high school but I loved certain topics more than others. For example, I liked Shakespeare and I wrote for the student newspaper. I liked seeing my name in print. That really was a big deal for me. I also liked to write to Amnesty International.

In my senior year of high school, I went with my friends to Greenwich Village. I saw all of the university kids. They looked so smart and were edgy. Yet they had little street smarts. I wanted to go to there; to be in those beautiful buildings.

"Is there a chance", I thought to myself? No, not me; I needed to go to community college instead. At one point I even wrote a personal statement applying to some schools, but most said no. I met with a few deans and they too said no. I kept trying. I thought, "I'm either going to get into school or I am going to get arrested".

Guess what? I got into a school. There was a dean who was particularly interested in my tenacity and my failures. He bet on me. He liked my resilience and humor I guess and eventually he gave me a scholarship to New York University, or NYU. He told me to just give back and I will never forget that. Everybody in his or her lives meets an angel and he was mine. He liked my story. He liked the genuine nature of what I had to say. He said, "Don't let me down". I ended up graduating with a 3.9 GPA. It was a strong lesson; when someone risks his job for you and says "Do not let me down". You never let him down. I still try to stick to that ethos today. Not for gratitude; it is just your word is your bond. Keep it.

During my time at school, I really got into my academics. I slept at Bobst Library. I joined the NYU debate team and the NYU philosophy Society. We sat in cafés and spent hours debating whether we exist or not; absurd, I know.

I also studied at the University of London for some time, studying British and Irish politics and Shakespeare. We used to go to Shakespeare's plays. I was literally living a dream life. It all would never have happened unless it was for that dean. NYU is now one of the top schools and I graduated in the top one percent. I am proud of that.

In my time there, I realized that the very wealthy kids had serious problems too. I always thought that they had it easy, but that's not always true. It was a learning experience for me. No matter where you come from, everybody has demons to deal with no matter how big their bank account is. That was the pre-educational spirit, jealousy and envy, of what drove me at first and matured into other motivations latter such as focusing on the means not the end. We all know what happens in the end.

Impact of My Father's Experience With The KGB And Life In The Soviet Union

It was the impact of my dad's experience with the KGB that led me to practice immigration law. My life experiences, whether they were good or bad, were quite dramatic for a young child. What it did, however, was it created an enormous amount of direction for me to devote oneself to one thing. It's not just you. You have to not only get your own life in order, but there are other people that need help as well.

One example that resonated with me, was another experience where my father saved $2,500 trying to buy a taxi in New York City. He ended up getting ripped off. The guy took everyone's money and left. It turned out he was a criminal and was involved in onerous crimes. We ended up going to court and that all affected me on many levels.

As a lawyer, one of the important things is that you have to feel like a guardian to your clients. You have to take care of them. You have to make sure that you do the best you can. Of course you cannot always do that. That would be a false statement. You just have to do your best, and let them know. Most clients appreciate when you work hard for them. Some of those negative experiences in life have made that very clear.

Impact Of Diverse Experiences On Legal Practice

NYU takes pride in being one of the international universities. Because of this I met people from all over the world during my time there. Before this, I had not had such exposure. It was not always positive; in fact it actually can make you a little lazy. I would fall asleep in the library a lot, reading Marx and Hegel and all the great philosophers. During that time, I learned there was no way I was going to compete with these kids even if I made certain amounts of money. They would always have more in their trust account than I could ever have; even if I worked twenty-four hours a day.

That was a dark period when I was at NYC, thinking I could not have ever competed with the world's elite. However, it was also a teachable moment. I realized you cannot envy anyone and you can't change anyone's trust account. What you need to do is focus on yourself and be the greatest possible lawyer you can be. That takes hard work and it takes losing sometimes. You may need to lose which can make you even better. If you aren't losing on occasions, you are not trying. You have to take risks and get your head bludgeoned by other attorneys some times.

While I was at NYC, I was the captain of the debate team. That too had a really profound effect on me. I started debating people from Yale, Princeton, and Harvard. I would win one or two matches and I felt I could compete with the big boys. After all, they were definitely groomed with congressional representatives as fathers and that sort of thing.

I knew when I stepped in the arena in a debate that I could summon my powers, my immigrant and blue collar experiences, and turn them into assets. They didn't see me coming. When you have nothing to lose, you become so much more liberated and you can do so much more. One important thing learned in those debate circles is to not be afraid to lose. It's actually very educational and what happens is, eventually you will start winning.

That was the influence of NYU; law school was a different animal though. People think law school is an extension of academics; it's not. It is a professional school. I applied to New York University, Pepperdine University, and New York Law School. At that time, I was an ultraliberal. I was following Nadine Strossen, the President of the American Civil Liberties Union. She had taught at NYU and I wanted to work for the ACLU being the ultraliberal that I was at the time. Once she moved to New York Law School, I wanted to do the same. I wanted to learn constitutional law from her. On a funny note, it turned out she didn't like me as a student. She thought I asked too many questions and she thought I was trying to be too smart. She used to destroy me in debates and we stood opposite on many issues but I still admired her. I thought being the president of the ACLU, in the United States, yielded an enormous amount of power. I learned so much from herrn so much from her. She did give me some sound advice. She said, "Follow your passion. Your passion and my passions are not the same but that doesn't mean one's better than the other." Being rebuffed by someone I looked up to, matured me in my law school days.

I later went on to Oxford University for a few semesters. I studied international law from Professor Craig. I also studied with a Supreme Court Justice from New Hampshire who was a guest lecturer. At that time, the European Union was starting to get together and constitute itself, so there I was studying international law, watching Professor Craig who was actually involved in putting it all together back then. We learned all about directives, the European Council, and the European bank.

That is when I was exposed to the Chair of Philosophy at NYU, who was a visiting fellow at Oxford at the time, Professor Paul Boghossian. He had an enormous amount of impact on my life.

It was he who actually challenged my ethnic identity. He told me to stop identifying with my Armenian ethnicity because it was really a social construct. He told me I was more of a human. We would have debates at the pub and in college for hours. I was following the Continental

Philosophy of Jacque Derrida and he was more into Bertrand Russell and Analytic Philosophy. We had these intellectual debates repeatedly and I held my own. I believed in armchair philosophy while he believed that the philosopher should wear a white coat. We went at it and it was an unbelievable time for me. You have to understand I was living a dream. Coming from my background, there weren't too many kids that were doing this. I felt a little special. Here I was dorming at Oxford, having dinner at the Inns of Court and meeting judges. It was heaven!

I felt very blessed, but with the blessings was the curse; the curse of guilt. Why was I making it in this amazing, prestigious world? Why was I sitting there in the courts of London, sitting next to the highest court judges, wearing black robes? This went beyond my comprehension. It was really a credit to how amazing America is. You will never hear me bash America. Sure it has some flaws, but I will tell you right now that for someone that came as a refugee to the United States to end up studying at Oxford, it was a blessing.

With this curse of guilt, I felt like the only way to give back was to make sure you have other kids goes experience what you did. You have to tell them that it's okay and that they can do it. There is nothing really stopping you. Many times, we live in ourselves too much. If you take those limits off yourself, it is unbelievable. You can unleash your power and optimism.

Look at me going to NYU. I went there eighteen times and would not take no for an answer. Maybe I was stubborn, or tenacious. I don't know. However, that type of tenacity got me into NYU and then into Oxford. It's the same type of tenacity you need in litigation and the same tenacity you need in court.

This doesn't mean you won't lose at trial. However, you keep trying. Juries like lawyers who want to win more than the other lawyer does. They see it and they feel it. In the end, those are the certain nuances that trial lawyers get.

University of Oxford

CHAPTER 3

ARE YOU OVERLY EMPATHETIC TO IMMIGRATION LAW CLIENTS?

As a lawyer, you have to be professional. You also have to be competent, diligent, knowledgeable, zealous, and highly compassionate. You have to have empathy towards your clients. However, when you look at them in an immigration case, they come not just as one client; they come as the whole family. You really see the family dynamics. When I see certain families, it reminds me of my own.

There was one instance where the client didn't have a wallet. He took out whatever was in his pocket; just a few dollar bills and rolled up pieces of paper. It kind of reminded me of my dad a little bit.

As the immigration attorney, you should see your family in your clients. When you're engaged and they pay you a retainer, which is their hard-earned money, you have to do your very best for them. You have to go above and beyond. That is not mere talk; a lot of it requires work. In some cases you may not be successful. You can't be one-hundred percent successful; that's rare. You have to prepare the clients for the best as well as the worst. You can't over inflate their expectations either because you are dealing with some very serious resourceful adversaries.

Although you see yourself in these people you still have to try to detach and just be a highly professional lawyer when you represent them. They are not looking for sympathy; they are very proud people. They are looking for a lawyer to do a good job.

In the end, results matter more than anything else. Besides that sort of ideology, and idealistic look, hard work is really the ultimate thing that gets the job done in most of these cases. Law is simple. Out-hustle, out-work your adversary and care more about your case and your client, and you will win most of the time. Judges know who cares more. They also know who cares about the money only. The jury studies the lawyers on both sides and the lawyer that relates to them the most and has his credibility intact at closing, usually wins!

THE UNIVERSAL DECLARATION
OF Human Rights
ADOPTED BY THE UNITED NATIONS GENERAL ASSEMBLY AT

CHAPTER 4

WHAT FACTORS HAVE INFLUENCED YOUR DECISIONS AS AN ATTORNEY?

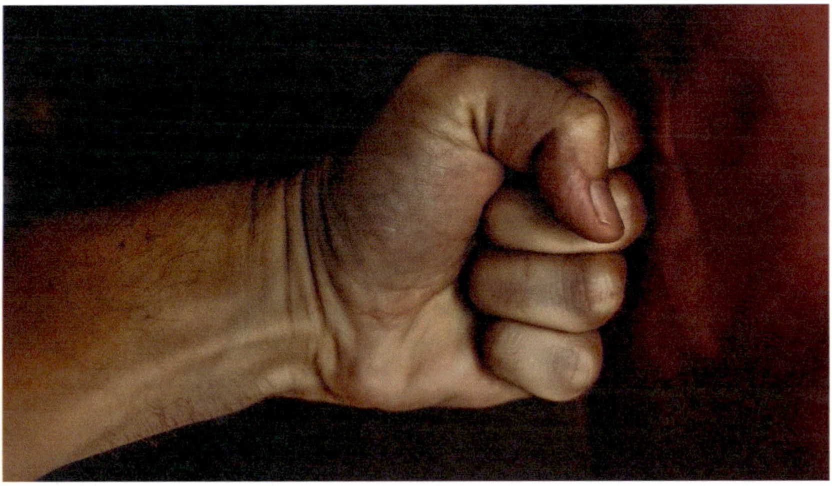

When I passed the bar and graduated law school, I sent out 800 resumes. I got a job as a legal recruiter for about a day. They asked me to call everyone in the yellow pages. One thing about the corporate world is you are nothing; zero. I was knocked down many pegs. It was a dose of reality. I walked off that legal recruiting job in about eight hours.

I then worked at a congressional law office for Congresswoman Marge Roukema who was dean of the New Jersey congressional delegation. I worked in the Ridgewood office in New Jersey and I did the academies. I basically appointed certain outstanding kids to go to the Air force Academy, the Naval Academy, West Point and to the Coast Guard. I did that for a year until I could find a job. I then realized I had a hidden love of politics. I used to drive Congresswoman Roukema at 5:00 in the morning and heard some very fascinating conversations during that time. I worked there for a year and then got a job at a small law firm in Bloomfield, New Jersey. I was told if I continued to act like a priest, I would be fired, so I had better start acting like a lawyer. I learned New Jersey law very quickly. That required a lot of aggression on my part. As a young lawyer all you have is aggression and energy, nothing else and you better use what you have.

The thought was to just use your aggression to get what you want, because your knowledge is very limited at this time. I really was bounced around quite a bit. I learned the ropes from some pretty tough lawyers. That toughened me up quite a bit. They viewed me as some soft lawyer and they said there was no room for that. I needed to shut up and make money. I did learn a lot though. I learned that aggression works for some people. I learned that you always have to learn the good and the bad. I would say that was a good experience.

Later, my father passing away had a very significant impact on my law career. When he died, he had paid $178 to buy life insurance from a large insurance company for which I cannot name. Unfortunately, he died before he got his medical examination. They denied his life insurance policy so I ended up going to ten different lawyers, asking if there was anything we could do. They all said we had no case; we were going to lose. I was a licensed attorney so I litigated the case on my own. I unleashed so much fury on this insurance company. In about four months, they gave a sizeable amount of money to me; I won the case. I used that settlement to pay my mother's mortgage and she gave me part of it to start my own practice. I never looked back after that.

The Author

CHAPTER 5
WHAT IMPACT DO YOUR METHODS AND PERSONALITY HAVE ON THE COURTROOM?

A good lawyer knows the law. He knows and prepares for cases and is able to show his adversaries and the judge that he is a professional who is doing a good job and is prepared. That's one dimension of it. The other dimension is a bit non-written. He always must show respect to the judge, regardless of the consequences. As far as an adversary is concerned, you always show respect to him as well. There is a requirement of civility in the courtroom. That doesn't mean you need to have sympathy for an adversary. Certain lawyers that do, I find troubling. That's my personal opinion.

As the attorney, you must be there to zealously represent your client. The word "zeal" is biblical; borderline it can mean acting to a point of being mentally ill. It's such an obsessive requirement to represent your client in such a zealous way; it's literally an ethical requirement. I don't think it is very zealous if you want to have drinks with your clients or your adversary in the middle of a case; I don't think it's ever a good idea. You shake hands, say hello and be civil but I do not think that your adversary is or your client is ever your best friend. You need to understand this is a very adversarial system, and you need to engage in advocacy; which requires you to be relentless, fearless, and prepared.

My personality over the years has changed in the courtroom. I used to get my head handed to me by senior lawyers. I bought into it when they would say things like, "Do you know who I am?"

At the time I would say, "I've heard of you", but that sort of thing doesn't affect me anymore. I don't really care who you are. I should be asking, "Do you know who I am?" I think that type of confidence makes you better in the courtroom.

I don't care anymore who the adversary is. They are going to deal with my tenacity, aggression, and intensity. If you aren't prepared for that, then I don't really care what firm you come from, or what person you think you are. You might have had a good case eight years ago but that doesn't make you a good lawyer now. I don't defer to so called "super lawyers". The truth is, everyone is subject to be beaten. That's the way I look at it. It's not for bragging purposes; it's in the best interest of your client. You cannot be intimidated by someone saying, "Do you know who I am?"

The bottom line is in the courtroom you are both lawyers who passed the bar exam; you are both equally matched. The courtroom is a great equalizer and the appellate division can be a greater equalizer. I was once up against one of the most prestigious law firms in New Jersey. It was a dispute over a pizzeria box payment. I represented the pizzeria owner. My opponent represented a large manufacturer of the pizza boxes. I looked up the lawyer and found he was a Colombia graduate and went to Harvard Law School. I thought this person must be amazing. We ended up going to trial. I realized, however, very quickly that he didn't know what he was doing. I didn't show any mercy in that situation. I had a chip on my shoulder about these Harvard law guys.

This attorney, in the middle of my trial, instead of objecting, he raised his hand. The judge said to him, "What are you doing?" He replied with, "What he's saying is wrong." The judge then said, "Why are you raising your hand? You're supposed to object."

I will never forget that. Apparently, even though he may have been bright and had good schooling, this guy had no trial advocacy skills. I am not demeaning him whatsoever, but sometimes practical skills matter. He could have simply objected, and said, "Let's have a side bar." Instead he raised his hand like if he was in the classroom.

I have an enormous amount of respect for Harvard lawyers; they are phenomenal. Nevertheless, that is just one example of one person that did not have the skills necessary to go to trial. Going to trial is different. It doesn't matter what school you attended. If you don't have trial experience, you aren't going to beat a trial lawyer. No trial lawyer is phenomenal from the beginning. It requires thousands of hours to be a master in the courtroom.

I am the voice of
the voiceless.
C.M. Punk

CHAPTER 6

DO JUDGES, PROSECUTORS AND INSURANCE COMPANIES VIEW A CASE DIFFERENTLY WHEN YOU SHOW UP FOR TRIAL?

I have to be honest. Martin Asatrian does not intimidate insurance companies and I would rather keep it that way. Insurance companies have unlimited resources. Losing a million dollars is nothing to them. They think they have this thing down to a science. I would rather insurance companies and adversaries underestimate me versus overestimate me. What happens is they get sloppy.

I'll give you an example. I was doing a legal malpractice case. The lawyer called me an idiot over the phone, and said, "Drop your case or you're going to lose you attorney fees".

Instead, because I worked on Sundays, I always sent him discovery demands on those days, only to remind him that I am working on the weekend while he is out playing golf. He ended up settling the case for a sizeable amount of money in less than a year.

Sometimes you need to be creative. I think to call somebody an idiot is not civil lawyering. He looked me and saw I was only four years out of law school and clearly tried to intimidate me. This guy had no idea how obsessed I became with this case after he toyed with my pride and the boulder on my shoulder. In this case, the boulder fell on him and on his client. It was the worst thing he could have done and it was the best thing that happened to me. It made me become obsessive with the case. I have to tell you all trial lawyers have chips on their shoulders. The best ones do. I may be carrying a boulder.

THE RIGHTS
OF MAN
ET DU CITOYEN

CHAPTER 7
WHAT IS THE FUTURE OF SOLO PRACTICE?

As far as the future of law is concerned in New Jersey and in New York the era of the solo practice is over. I said this at a speech at the Chamber of Commerce and I got some interesting feedback. The majority of lawyers in America are solo practitioners and I believe that their days are numbered. I think they should collaborate with larger firms or else they are not going to meet their overhead. The costs of doing business in a solo practice are increasing; filing fees, rent, and labor. Retainers are not in conjunction with these rising costs.

They are going to end up transitioning into other areas of the economy and not practice law. I know a lot of dissatisfied solo practitioners who are always complaining. Nevertheless, I am not a big person on complaining because it's hard to complain when you live in America and you're a white male. You need to adapt and I think many of these solo practitioners need to do just that.

There are many attorneys that are still doing very well and still working in a high capacity at older ages. If you are 84 and still practicing law I think that's a wonderful thing. I always wonder though if maybe you should slow it down a little bit. There are many people who are still practicing into their nineties and it's fine but are they giving the best amount of legal representation to their clients? I don't know. I hope that doesn't sound like ageism. I wish I could be a lawyer and practice law into my 90s. I also know if my skills are diminishing it might be time to move on.

The second thing is other than the diminishing of the solo practice is the role of money in law and the access to the courts. I don't know how the small business owner can compete with the monster corporation who can higher large firms in a dispute and how that could be equitable. The candy store owner can't afford a $180,000 in legal fees without going bankrupt, while a manufacturer can throw away millions of dollars and not have a problem.

There I see the greatest inequity in civil litigation. The larger firms are going to win many cases not based on the merits necessarily, but rather they taper another lawyer to death. They can write motion after motion and do deposition after deposition. They can afford to hire the most expensive experts. I don't know how a sole practitioner can keep up with that. Sole practitioners cannot underwrite litigation where they put out the fees of $80,000, for example, hoping to win the case. Let's say they do that for five cases; that's $400,000. How are they going to afford that especially if they lost all five cases? They will go bankrupt. The larger firms have larger credit lines whereas a lot of smaller firms cannot get credit lines. Again, there is this is a huge disparity in money.

Unfortunately, the last thing that we did not talk about is the merit. If you cannot reach the merits because procedurally you are going to be bludgeoned by a larger firm, it is going to be very difficult for solos to survive.

By the way, solo practitioners are tenacious, amazing, brilliant lawyers. However, the problem is economically and financially, I don't know how, for example, with the costs of medical technologies in personal injury cases, you could afford to bring in medical experts. It would cost you cost you $30,000 to $50,000 for each case, and that might not be worth more than $15,000 in a settlement.

I believe the future of law is that solo practitioners will need to join larger personal injury firms that have certified civil trial attorney status and that have the wherewithal, the offices, the army of lawyers that you will need to survive in a highly competitive legal market. The way of the future is simply power in numbers. Solo personal injury lawyers will be well served to join larger personal injury firms in order to balance the playing field. This is the trend. It will continue to grow so that lawyers can argue cases more on the merits and less on ability to finance a case.

All of these solos are going to unite into a larger law firm, and I think they will be very happy for it. I would encourage that, because there is power in numbers. For example, if you have a hundred solo practitioners uniting in a larger personal injury firm that's going to be good for everyone. I hope that's the case in the future, because at the end of the day, the person who wins and earns is the client. The client doesn't want to lose, especially because your firm didn't have enough money to pay for experts. They may be willing to lose because maybe they were wrong or maybe I was their fault; not for any reasons involving financial economics.

United Nations
Human Rights

OFFICE OF THE HIGH COMMISSIONER FOR HUMAN RIGHTS

CHAPTER 8
HOW WAS YOUR EXPERIENCE AS A POLICE COMMISSIONER?

I moved to Englewood Cliffs, NJ at one point because that's where my dad and I used to sell hot dogs to some of the richer kids. I suppose that it is the chip on my shoulder speaking. After my house was flooded, I went to a local mayor council meeting and asked if they could do anything. A council member, now deceased, shouted at me that night. He talked down to me in front of everybody. I responded in kind, reminded him I was a lawyer but he didn't care. A few people in the party approached me, and wanted me to run for office so I ended up running for a council position and won. I was elected to Englewood Cliffs Council where I ended up serving as the Police Commissioner.

It wasn't day-to-day police work but had more to do with budgeting and things of that nature. It was interesting experience though especially coming from my background. It's important to understand Englewood Cliffs is one of the richest zip codes in the United States. The average house has to be worth over $800,000 minimum. I had a brief exposure to being a council member here. I made some good friends and tried to do the best I could. Again, it's one of those things that Barrack Obama used to talk about, "Only in America". I think there is no greater cheerleader for the American Dream than me.

A Migrant Mother

CHAPTER 9
HOW WAS YOUR EXPERIENCE AS AN ADJUNCT PROFESSOR?

I always wanted to be an adjunct professor. A rabbi came up to me when I was working at my dad's gas station in New Jersey and said, "I've seen you reading a lot. What's your deal?"

I said, "I have a decision to make. I can either become a lawyer or get my PhD in French philosophy."

He said to me, "How much money would you make as a professor?"

I said, "Well, I would be a teacher's assistant so I would probably make about $35,000."

He then said, "How much money would you make as a lawyer?"

I said, "Probably about $75,000."

He said, "You've probably answered your own question."

I also had a cab driver who told me he had a PhD in French philosophy and he was now driving cab in New York. That frightened me a lot. There is nothing wrong with it and this guy might have been happier than most lawyers I know. However, I didn't want to be a PhD in French philosophy, and driving a cab. I was trying to be a little more practical than that.

The irony was law gave me the opportunity to teach at the university level as an adjunct professor, where maybe a PhD might not have. I taught American government, constitutional law, business law, forensic science, and some criminal law. I loved it. Being a professor, standing there in front of the future, you get a jury in a sense. It sharpens your trial skills exponentially. There is no question about it. It also shows you how deficient you are. You know instantly if they are not happy with your class. You can see their eyes roll and so you have to change your rhythm. You have to give them more important and interesting topics. You have to be quick on your feet as an attorney but as a professor, you have to be quick on your feet as well. You don't want to bore your students to death; you want to give them fascinating content.

Life is short and because my dad died at a very young age, I was trying to rush a lot off my bucket list. I was doing everything; counseling, teaching, law, and traveling. I was just trying to do as much as I could in a short period. I thought my expiration date was sixty-three, the age my dad died, and I still have that in my head.

I also went on to a seminary for three years. Practicing law, teaching, and traveling to over thirty countries, was not enough, my greedy eyes wanted more. I wanted to turn the clock back and I wondered why my parents did not instill in me or my siblings a sense of spirituality. Instead, it was all materialism. I felt my parents' worldview was not that much different than Karl Marx. Sometimes my dad was a Marxist capitalist, if that makes any sense. He hated communism but sometimes sure acted like a Marxist. Was religion truly the opiate of the masses?

Karl Marx

CHAPTER 10
THE SEMINARY EXPERIENCE

I have a spiritual dimension to me. This whole like dying young thing scared me so much. I just wanted to do everything. While people were out partying on Friday nights while I was reading about Jonah and the whale and Daniel in the lion's den. I went from Genesis all the way through Revelations in about three years. I wrote papers on it and I received a ministry degree. Some people will disrespect me for it, so I keep that very close to the vest.

Honestly though studying the bible does enhance your relationship with your clients. It puts things into perspective on a cosmic consciousness level. I get a great sense of calmness and internal peace through my Christian faith. I also get the same from people like Eckhart Tolle and the Omega Institute (Zen Buddhism). I really like Buddhism so I conjoined Zen Buddhism and Christianity which are generally not much different. I find the teachings of Christ have been so misinterpreted by so many people, but that's probably for another book. I will say one thing, Christ, as far as law is concerned, added a dimension in the sermon that law is great. However, we need to go beyond that. Whatever the law is, you need to go above it, because it is the right thing to do. I believe he called it grace.

Interestingly enough, the seminary allowed me to humble myself and it knocked me down a few pegs. My law practice changed a bit from these experiences and it tempered my aggression and helped me focus on humility. Clients are drawn to humility and selflessness. Some lawyers see a client and they begin counting the dollars. The better ones see a story, a problem, and see how they can fix it or simply decide and admit they cannot fix i. Clients are very astute and they sense when a lawyer is being sincere or when he is simply being a glorified salesman.

My deepest takeaway from studying the bible and finding home in my protestant roots is that no matter how hard we think we have it, in the course of history, we are just fine. If anyone is tormented by anxiety and fear of a premature death, find a bible, go to church, an ashram, whatever. Unplugging from society and experiencing solitude is time well spent. Seneca talked about the preoccupied life and the leisured life. Somehow we need to strike a balance. I have to admit, that with having a four year old, the leisured life is out the window for now. However, I am trying to live a life, so I can give my boy, Benjamin, nice clothes, good schools, fun vacations and nice birthday parties. For now, I may have to scrap the leisured life and focus on making a living. However, nevertheless the seminary taught me a sense of fearlessness and gave me a comfort with my own mortality.

Supreme Court of the United States of America

CHAPTER 11
HOW DO YOU SEE THE FUTURE OF IMMIGRATION LAW?

I have practiced immigration law under the George W. Bush era, through the Obama era and up until now during this new administration. There is one thing that I can advise and that is if you have a green card and you are eligible to be a naturalized citizen, then you need to hire an immigration lawyer and become a U.S. citizen. Get a United States passport, because then the (DHS), the Department of

Homeland Security, will have no jurisdiction over you. There are many people with green cards out there that are not filing and I don't know why. Right now is definitely the environment to do this. That is one piece of advice I can give. So study for the test. It's not that hard. You will pass and then you will get citizenship. More and more lawyers should encourage that.

Second, I do not know how you can have a father or a mother take a two year old across the border from Mexico to the United States. That two year old grows up in New Jersey and goes to high school, plays football, gets a scholarship, and one day wants to join the military. They are really part of the American fabric. I don't know how that person can be subject to removal from a moralistic standpoint. I can certainly see it from a legalistic standpoint. However, some of these kids go to college. They want to join the military and are willing to die for their country – to give the ultimate sacrifice.

One example of this is a person who came from the Soviet Union as an immigrant in the late seventies. I believe he was a refugee. He went to Stamford University and was a cofounder of probably the most important company ever, Google. His name is Sergey Brin. Those are some of the opportunities that we may be missing when we remove people. How many more Sergey Brins are out there that we may be deporting! Don't get me wrong. If you commit a heinous act and you are here without status, it's a hard argument to make that you should stay in the United States. I don't support that whatsoever.

However, I do support those innocent people out there without criminal records, who are doing the best they can. What about the Sergey Brins who create so many jobs in America and give so much prestige to this country from an innovation standpoint? How many Sergey Brins are there that we are not respecting right now? There is a lot of brain power in the world. One innovation can really transform everything. Brilliant minds can be cultivated in our universities and we should be embracing all types of people. There is a big delineation between heinous criminal acts and people who have no criminal records. I think that logic can really delineate between those two types of people.

Immigration is highly complex. For example, there are a lot of U.S workers that feel like their jobs are being taken and that is a legitimate argument. They don't want to be displaced by someone who came here illegally. At the same time, there could be a way where it would be a win-win for everybody. It's going to take a great mind and leadership to get us to that point and we will.

Don't be surprised if we get amnesty in the United States because people are realizing that it is very hard to remove 11 million people. It would require enormous amounts of resources. I am optimistic. Ronald Reagan was the most conservative president whom my dad loved and he gave us amnesty in 1986!

The more brilliant minds we have in the United States, the better. Everyone can contribute and I think that is in line with the 'American Dream'. When someone says, "I'm third generation", I say "Yes! You are sons of immigrants." In fact there is the gigantic cliché that we are all immigrants. We should all have some respect and decency for all families who are contributing to the U.S. fabric. That's my position and I know there are greater minds than mine out there figuring this all out.

We are the most generous country in the world. We can do this. We just need to take the negative emotion out of the equation.

IMMIGRATION
BUILT
THIS NATION

CHAPTER 12
HOW DID GROWING UP IN A BLUE COLLAR NEIGHBORHOOD IMPACT YOUR PERSONALITY?

We first moved to North Bergen in New Jersey, which is more of an immigrant community; mostly Cuban, and Dominican. A neighboring town was more blue collar. When I went to school, some of the parents of the students were truckers or were members of the carpenters' union. Others were police officers or maybe postal workers. They were working in what could be called blue collar jobs. What you learn from people like that, is a bit different than what you learn growing up in an immigration community. The blue collar communities were incredibly hospitable to my family. We made friends quickly.

What you realize is that their families suffered just as your family suffered. In addition, it was all about survival, but it didn't affect anyone's happiness. I found that very interesting. No matter what, when you do not understand deprivation, you still understand family.

In our family, the greatest delicacy was on Saturday morning when my dad would put us in his yellow cab and we would go to McDonald's. This pretty much became a precursor to law for me. I saw how hard my father and mother worked for us. I saw how it was my obligation to fulfill many of their dreams, which I am in a process of doing now.

My dad always instilled in us honesty and truthfulness. He said he came here and wanted us to flourish and be happy. That was not necessarily about money but I think it was also about a deeper freedom.

There is a definition of happiness that has more to do with liberty and freedom.

A lot of my close friends have bought homes in affluent suburbs and have nice jobs. I visit them and I wonder if they feel like they have arrived. I wish they would strive more. Life is not over at 45 just because you have a nice house, a nice car, a pool and you play golf. There is more to be done. Let us not stop pushing for greatness. In short, let us keep striving until the grave. This whole early retirement nonsense is overrated. Drive harder. Work harder. Stay hungry. That is the name of the game in law. I know a very successful personal injury lawyer who is killing it at 73. Keep learning and keep hustling. It really could be the real fountain of youth.

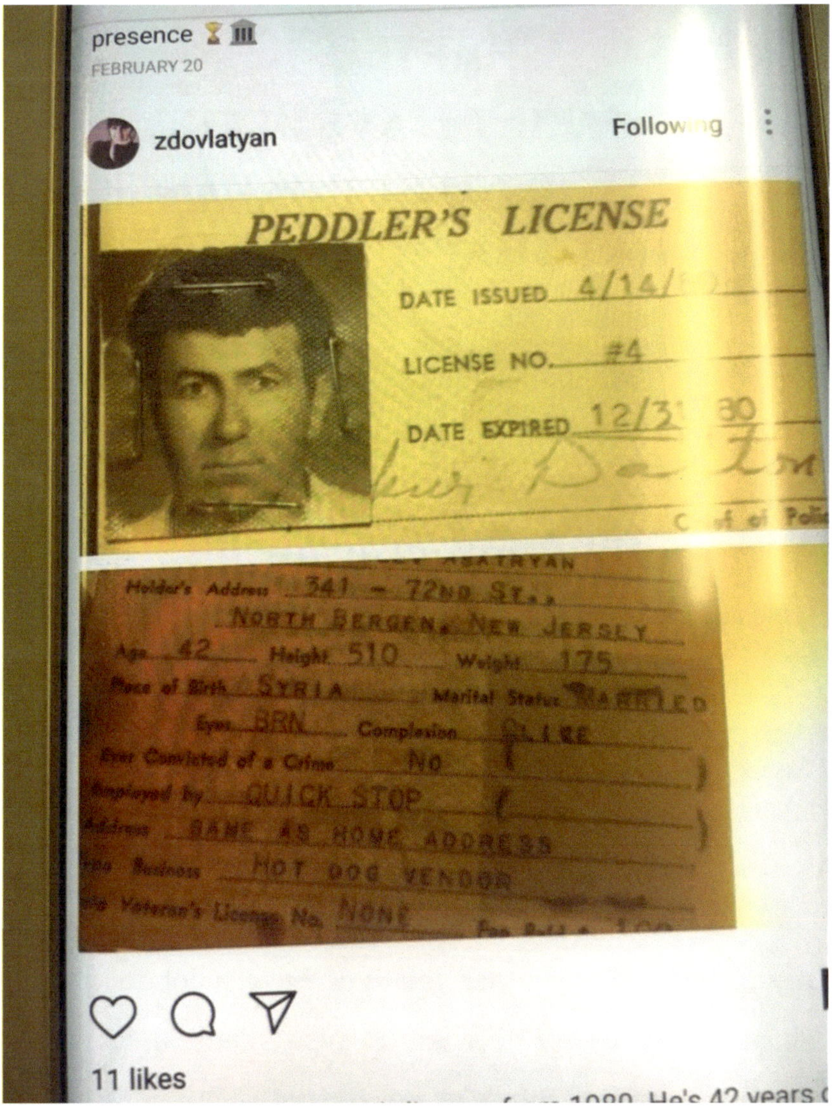

Peddler's License Issued In 1980

CHAPTER 13

WHAT HAVE BEEN THE GREATEST INFLUENCES THAT SHAPED YOUR LIFE?

I want to say thank you to my family. My brother, my sister and my other relatives have a lot to do with shaping my career. I want to also thank a lot of my existing, past and future clients for putting their faith in an attorney to help them in legal matters.

I want to say that the most important thing in the world really is gratitude. If we could just be more grateful for everything we have, I think it will put things in perspective.

As far as why I wrote this book, it's really for my son Benjamin, who is four. He definitely is the light of my life. I hope that he can read this book one day and understand where his father and his grandfather came from and what we went through. Maybe it will give him some insight and guide him as to how his father made mistakes or made some good moves. It may affect his decision-making. I wish all fathers could write some type of book or some type of a memo to their children about what they have gone through. I hope as an incidental benefit from this book, that my child can grow up, read it, understand it, question it, and maybe even criticize it. I hope it can also give an insight to his grandfather, who he never met. Many people do not understand it is extremely important to understand where you come from.

Additionally I have a serious aversion to mass deportations. Starting in the 19th century mass deportations led to genocide. In the middle of the 19th century, they led to the holocaust. I am concerned about these mass deportations and the impact they have on communities. I hope we can get the right people to understand that simple solutions are not the answer. Sometimes complexity requires more complexity. The solution may be highly complex and it may require a committee of people to understand that. I hope whoever reads this book, understands where I am coming from.

I'm not saying that my life is anything special, but I want to share part of my life with the reader. I want to let them know that this is one human, who is expressing his life experiences to another human. You can leave your hometown and have the most amazing experiences. My travels throughout the world, going to Uzbekistan when I was six years old, or to Georgia when I was seven, that's just a life situation that happened to me. It does not make me better or worse. However, it definitely has an impact on the way I practice law and the way I look at life.

The greatest impact on my life has been the people that told me you can't do this or that. Well, how do they know? I learned negative people kill dreams and aspirations. If you have negativity in your life, get rid of it quick. If you complain to others and they join in your complaints, get rid of them too. Here, is hint, if you are the poorest person in your circle, you are hanging out with the right people. Success rubs off and unfortunately does failure.

Keeping Families Together

WHAT IS THE NEXT STEP?

At age 45, the next step is to hopefully write more books and utilize my skills and experience to help as many clients as I can in the area of immigration and personal injury law. Both are very complex and very labor intensive areas of the law. From a numerical standpoint, the next five years, which will be 2022, I would like to have successfully represented over 1,000 clients. I plan on working on Saturdays with one day of rest. I also want to give educational talks on Univision, Cable TV, and Social Media to reach as many people as possible.

On a professional level, I would like to create a conglomerate of attorneys throughout the country to help each other, and in turn help clients as well. I would like to focus on helping immigrants the most right now, as there is great suffering in that area of law. It bothers me on a cellular level when I see the government try to deport parents when they have children who are U.S. citizens. Keeping families together is the so important.

As you can tell I want to touch as many lives as I can in my law practice and would like to partner up with like minded professionals. At the same time, I cherish my solitude and enjoy my time communing with the Lord. Sometimes as lawyers we do God’s work. Let us keep up that tradition. Who knows, if I play my cards right, I can be nominated as a judge one day!

ACKNOWLEDGEMENTS

I want to acknowledge all of those that inspired me to write this book. First and foremost, I want to thank my clients who have put their trust in me over the years to serve them to best of my abilities. I would also like to name some of the people who have stood by me as I wrote this letter. I would like to thank the following and in no particular order; my parents, my family, my son, Benjamin Asatrian, Lisa Grazioso, Harry Asatrian, Hasmik Asatrian, my nephews, nieces, and relatives that have joined us in our journey in the United States.

I want to thank certain colleagues that have been instrumental in promoting my career including Congresswomen Marge Roukema, Robert Bianchi, Stan Fishman, Paul Weiner, Andy Aslanian, Eric Kahn, and all of the lawyers at the great firm of Javerbaum Wurgaft, P.C.

I would also like to thank certain outstanding influences on my career, Benedict Morrelli, who in a brief time taught me the importance in balancing aggression and compassion in the court room.

I want to thank my dear friends; Connie Barrera, Grizel Campos, Danielle Sapporito, and Jay Kanetkar.

I also would like to thank people who have inspired me to write this book and encouraged me to get my story out. I would like to thank my teachers, professors, and others who have given me great encouragement; J.D. Morgan, Paul Boghossian, Bertell Ollman, Timothy Mitchell, and to my friends Steve Vosbikian, my brother Harry Asatrian, and the memory of former Immigration Judge William F. Strasser, retired Judge Joseph Conte, retired Judge Don Venezia, and all other great influences in my life. Above all, I want to thank God for giving me life and everything in it.

INDEX

M

N

O

P

R

S

T

U

Z

NOTES

I want to make the following notes as an explanation for this book. I want to make it clear that with this book we pay homage to all the immigrants that came to the United States and help build this great country.

I want to apologize for any typographical errors, or the choppy nature of the book, I just wanted to make the point. That with the right immigration policies, our country could prosper and grow even better than ever. The 21st Century is the American Century.

Made in the USA
Monee, IL
05 November 2026

67386571R00055